A DISCOVERING SCIENCE BOOK

EXPLORING YOUR SKELETON

Funny Bones and Not-So-Funny Bones

By Pamela R. Bishop ∘ Illustrated by Liz Callen

FRANKLIN WATTS

New York   London   Toronto   Sydney
1991

For Ed, Shannyn, Ryan, and Blair.
And for all young children who are explorers
and scientists by their very nature.

—P. R. B.

Photograph on page 10 courtesy of Photo Researchers,
Inc./James Stevenson.

Library of Congress Cataloging-in-Publication Data

Bishop, Pamela R.
Exploring your skeleton : funny bones and not-so-funny bones / by
Pamela R. Bishop : illustrated by Liz Callen.
p.   cm.—(A Discovering science book)
Summary: Describes the appearance and functions of bones, their
association with muscles, tendons, and platelets, and how bones make
up the skeleton.
ISBN 0-531-10970-4
1. Musculoskeletal system—Anatomy—Juvenile literature.
[1. Bones. 2. Skeleton.] I. Callen, Liz, ill. II. Title.
III. Series.
QM100.B57   1991
611'.7—dc20   90-31026 CIP AC

Design by Barbara Powderly

Funny Bones and Not-So-Funny Bones

Have you heard about your funny bone? It's not funny at all. It is a place at the back of your elbow. When you hit it against something, it causes a tingling in your arm and hand. Now you know why it is also called our crazy bone.

Your funny bone isn't even a bone. It is the point where your lower and upper arm bones meet. The bone of your upper arm is called the *humerus* (HYOO-mer-uhs). Maybe this is why some people think our sense of humor comes from our funny bone. What do you think?

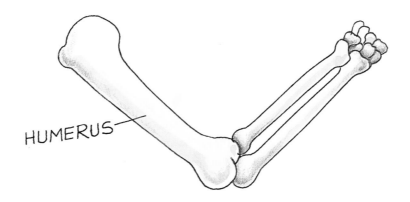

HUMERUS

Your *skeleton* (SKEL-e-tuhn) is made of many bones. Bones are what give you shape. If you had no bones you could not stand or sit. You would be like a jellyfish or a ball of clay.

When you were a baby, you had more than 300 bones. As you grow, some of these bones join together. When you are fully grown, you will have 206 bones in all.

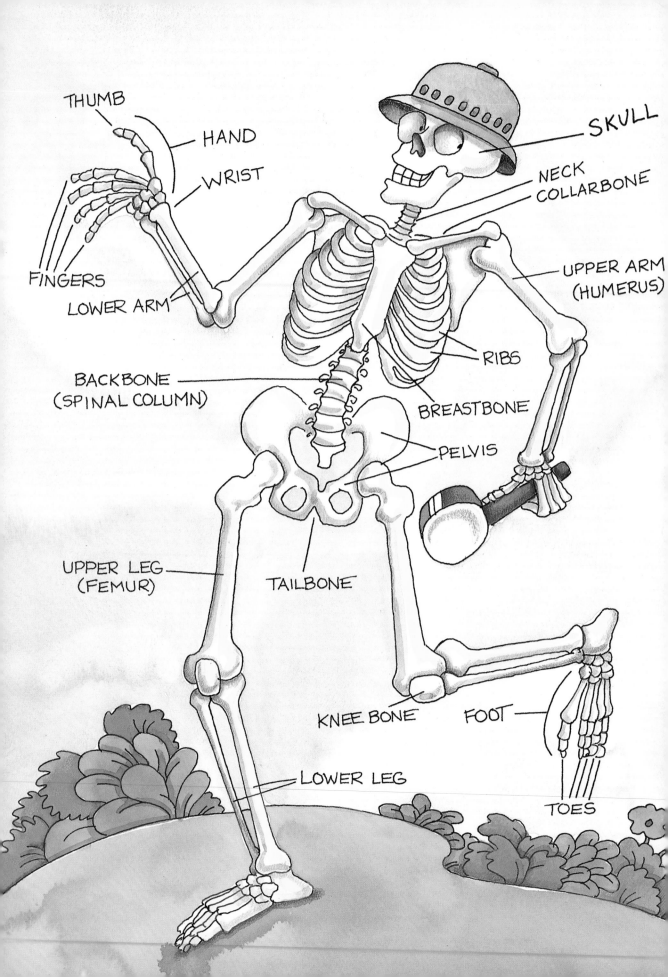

You have bones of all shapes and sizes in your skeleton. There are large, round bones like the humerus in your upper arm, or the *femur* (FEE-mer) in your upper leg. There are also very small bones in your fingers and toes. Some of your bones are flat, like the bones in your *skull* (SKUHL).

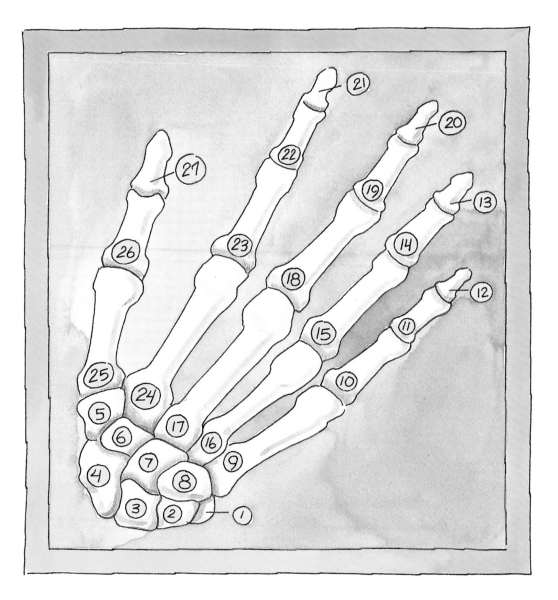

Nearly one-fourth of the bones in your body are found in your hands. Did you know that there are twenty-seven bones in each of your hands? Each finger, including your thumb, has three bones. Try and feel the bones in your hands. Count the bones in the drawing above.

Soft Bones, Hard Bones

Some of your bones are soft and some are hard. The bones that are very soft are called *cartilage* (KART-uh-lij). The bones in your ears and nose are cartilage. That's why you can bend back the top of your ear. That's why you can push the end of your nose flat. Try it. It doesn't hurt and it doesn't break.

But most of your bones are not soft cartilage. Most of your bones are hard. Sometimes the hard bones do break. You can fall down wrong on a bone and break it. A broken bone is called a *fracture* (FRAK-chuhr).

A doctor has to take a picture of the bone to see the fracture. This picture is called an X *ray* (X-rey). X rays can show the bone right through the skin.

Many fractures have to be set back together by a doctor. The doctor puts a *cast* (KAST) on it to keep the bone still while it grows back together. Sometimes you even need a sling to keep the bone from moving until it heals.

Joints, Tendons, and Ligaments

The place where one bone meets another is called a *joint* (JOYNT). A joint connects two bones together like a hinge on a door. The hinge lets the door open and close. The joints in your skeleton allow your bones to move in many ways.

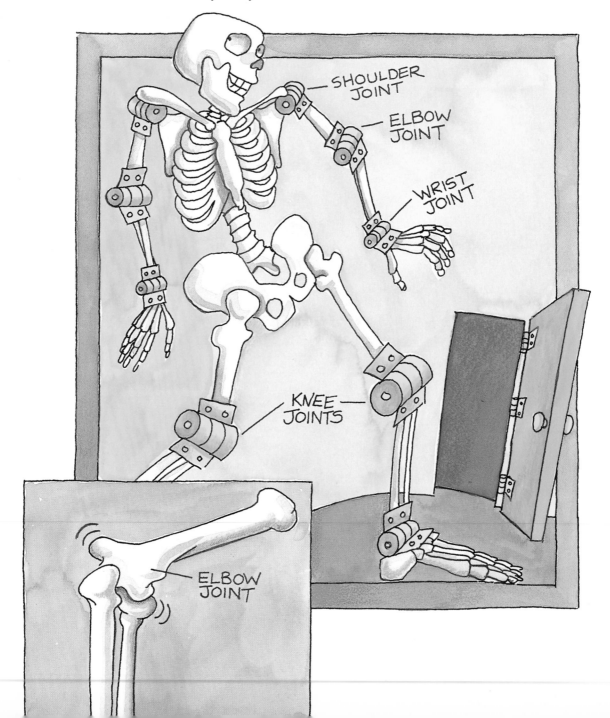

SHOULDER JOINT

ELBOW JOINT

WRIST JOINT

KNEE JOINTS

ELBOW JOINT

You have joints wherever you can twist and bend. You have joints in your neck, shoulders, elbows, and wrists. You also have joints in your hips, knees, ankles, and even in your toes. The joint in your jaw lets you open and close your mouth to talk and eat.

JAW

Having more than 200 joints in your body helps you move in many fun ways. You can hop like a kangaroo or tiptoe like a cat. You can climb and hang from a jungle gym or bend down to tie your shoes.

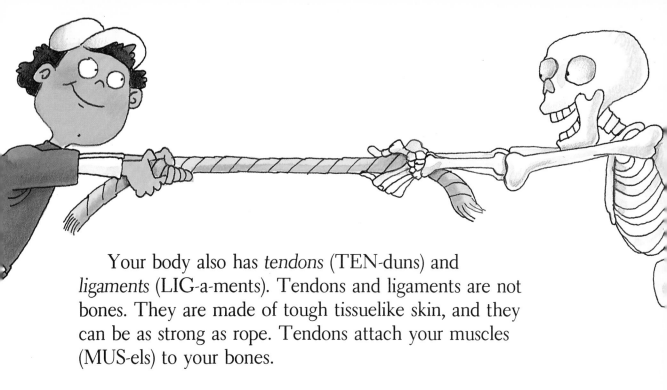

Your body also has *tendons* (TEN-duns) and *ligaments* (LIG-a-ments). Tendons and ligaments are not bones. They are made of tough tissuelike skin, and they can be as strong as rope. Tendons attach your muscles (MUS-els) to your bones.

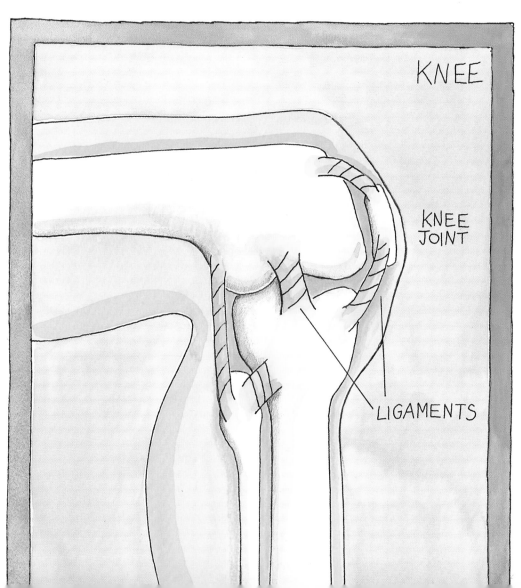

KNEE

KNEE JOINT

LIGAMENTS

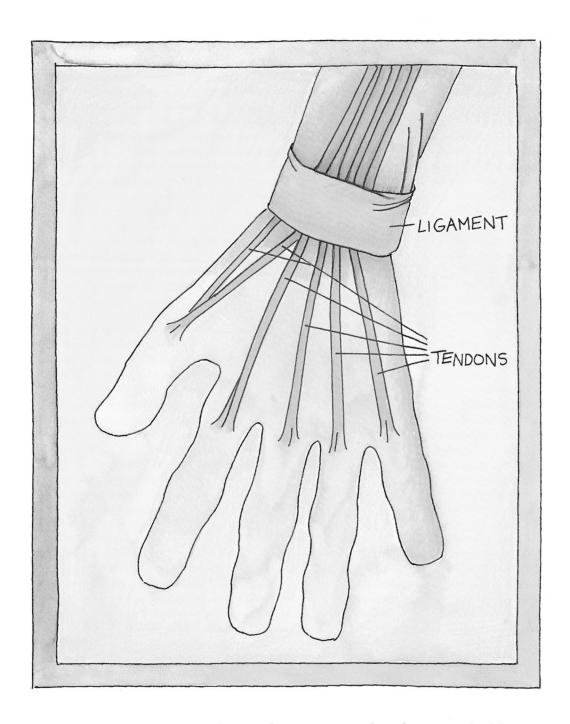

Ligaments attach one bone to another bone or hold a group of bones together. The tendons and ligaments in your hand are like rubber bands holding all the bones and joints together and connecting them to your arm.

Have you ever sprained your ankle? You have a *sprain* (SPRAYN) when a joint is twisted suddenly. This causes the ligaments to stretch too far or to tear. The doctor may tell you to keep your ankle still and let it heal by itself.

Super Bones!

How did your bones get to be so big? How do you get even taller than you are now?

Your bones grow. When you were a baby, you first had to learn to crawl. Then your bones got stronger and you could walk. Now you are bigger, but soon you will grow even more. You will be even taller and stronger.

Like the rest of your body, bones need food to grow and stay hard and strong. The best food for your bones is a body mineral called *calcium* (KAL-see-um). Calcium is in milk and dairy products, such as ice cream and cheese.

Your bones need calcium the whole time you are growing. If you eat or drink something with calcium in it every day, you will grow up with strong, healthy bones.

Bone Marrow: The Blood Cell Factory

Have you ever looked inside a steak bone? The hollow, spongy area you see is filled with soft bone *marrow* (MAR-row). Your bones are also filled with marrow.

Bone marrow is the "factory" where *blood cells* (BLUHD SELS) are made. Red blood cells, white blood cells, and *platelets* (PLAYT-lets) are parts of your blood.

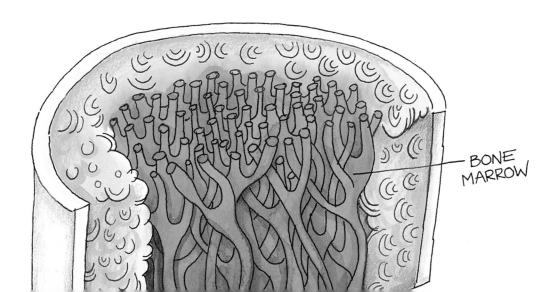

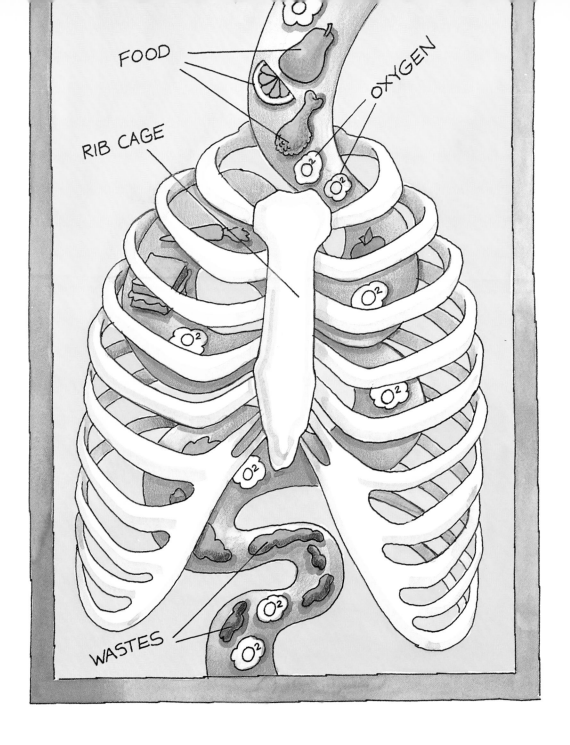

FOOD

OXYGEN

RIB CAGE

WASTES

The blood moves food and oxygen to all the parts of your body. It also brings germs and wastes out of your body to keep you well. Your bone marrow makes all this possible.

The Amazing Backbone

You have a special bone called the backbone. It is not just one bone. Your backbone is a column of thirty-three bones stacked one on top of another with joints in between.

All creatures with a backbone or central column of bone are called *vertebrates* (VER-tuh-brehts). You are a vertebrate.

People are not the only vertebrates. Dogs and cats, too, have backbones, and so do fish and birds. Reptiles such as alligators, and mammals, such as zebras and elephants, have a central column of bones. They are all vertebrates.

Creatures without a backbone or central column of bones are called *invertebrates* (in-VER-tuh-brehts). A jellyfish does not have a backbone. Neither do worms or snails. They are all invertebrates.

It would not be much fun to be an invertebrate. Without your backbone, you could not stand, sit, or play. Without it you could not bend over to pick up a ball, or run to ride your skateboard. You could only wiggle like a worm.

A Suit of Armor

Your skeleton is like a suit of armor. It protects your brain, heart, lungs, and other important parts of your body from danger.

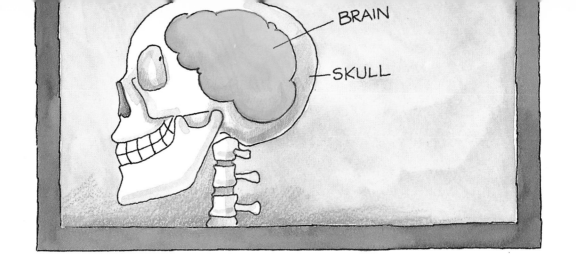

Your head bone, or *skull*, is like a cage that protects your brain from any hard bumps. The bones around your eyes help protect your eyes, too. Your *ribs* form a strong cage to protect your heart and lungs. Without these bones, you would get hurt easily.

Digging Up Old Bones

Bones last a long time after a person dies. Part of the work of scientists called *archaeologists* (ar-KEY-ol-uh-jists) is to dig up the bones of people who lived long ago. Archaeologists put the bones back together very carefully like a puzzle.

They piece the bones back together until they have a skeleton. From this skeleton they can see what early men and women looked like. They can tell how they walked, how they ate, and how they lived. Now you know how skeletons help us to learn about life on earth thousands, even millions, of years ago!

Exploring Your Skeleton

Without your skeleton, you would not be who you are. Your skeleton gives you shape. It has joints so that you can bend and wiggle your toes. It has a backbone so that you can stand and sit up straight and tall. It forms cages so that your insides are protected from harm. It makes the blood cells that help keep you alive. Best of all, it has a funny bone, too!

GLOSSARY

Archaeologist. A person who digs up bones and other clues about the past

Backbone. A central column of thirty-four bones stacked one on top of another

Blood cells. The structures blood is made of

Bones. Parts of hard tissue that form our skeleton

Brain. Place of intelligence, located in the skull

Calcium. A chemical needed for strong bones

Cartilage. Soft bone

Cast. A hard mold to keep broken bones in place while healing

Femur. The thighbone

Fracture. A broken bone

Funny bone. A part of the elbow

Humerus. The upper arm bone

Invertebrate. Creature without a backbone

Joint. Connects two or more bones

Ligament. A band of tough tissue that connects a bone to another bone

Marrow. The soft part inside the bones where blood cells are made

Muscle. A body tissue that makes body movement possible

Platelets. The part of the blood that controls how much you bleed when cut

Ribs. The bone cage that protects our heart and lungs

Skeleton. Our framework of bones

Skull. The bone cage that protects our brain

Tendon. A band of tough tissue that connects a muscle to a bone

Vertebrate. Creature with a backbone

X ray. Photograph taken of bones inside our body

About the Author
Pamela R. Bishop has taught science in the primary grades for over seven years. She holds a B.S. in Early Childhood Education from Martha Washington College and lives in Stafford, Virginia. This is her first picture book.

About the Artist
Liz Callen's work has appeared in numerous text books and trade books. She was educated at the Art Center College of Design in Los Angeles. She lives in Sebastopol, California, with her husband and three cats, two of which appear in this book.